海水为什么是咸的

Sharing the Planet | Non-Fiction Series

Copyright © 2022 by Level Learning, INC. and Washington Yu Ying PCS™
Original and Edited Text Copyright © 2022 by Washington Yu Ying PCS™

All rights reserved. No part of this book in whole or part may be reproduced without written permission from the publisher.

Published by Level Learning, INC.
Content Contributors:
Washington Yu Ying PCS™ - Qianyi (Shirley) Zhang, Pearl Zao He You
Level Learning - Jingyao Qi

Illustrations by: Josh Taira

Leveling classification based on Level Learning standard.
For full description, visit www.levellearning.com

ISBN 978-1-64040-057-3
Simplified Chinese Edition

About Level Learning:
Level Learning provides a literacy focused curriculum specifically designed for K-12 Chinese as a Second Language classrooms. Our program offers 20 levels of specific and detailed objectives, leveled texts and passages, mastery-based online assessment, and analytics to enable data-driven instruction. Level Learning reading curriculum for both literature and informational text emphasize grammar and comprehension skills to help teachers develop confident and independent Chinese language readers. The non-fiction series of books are specifically designed to support our informational text course based on multiple national standards. To learn more about our entire offering, visit www.levellearning.com.

About Washington Yu Ying PCS™:
Washington Yu Ying PCS is a Mandarin English dual language immersion International Baccalaureate (IB) World school. Yu Ying's mission is to inspire and prepare young people to create a better world by challenging them to reach their full potential in a nurturing Chinese/English educational environment. Yu Ying's comprehensive IB, dual immersion curriculum equips students with global competencies for success in the real world. As a leader in immersion education, Yu Ying is determined to advance Chinese language programs and global citizenry education by helping other schools create and strengthen their Chinese programs. For more information, email: products@washingtonyuying.org

为什么海水是咸的呢？下雨的时候，岩石和土壤里会有一点点的盐溶解出来。这些盐会被大大小小的河流带入海洋。

慢慢地,海水不断蒸发,可是盐还留在海水里。就这样,海水里的盐变得越来越多,海水就变咸了。

海水里的盐度越高,浮力就越大。

世界上有个神奇的地方叫死海。不会游泳的人也可以躺在死海的水面上，不会沉下去！这是因为死海的盐度很高，浮力也就非常大。

我们来做个实验吧。把一杯海水放在太阳下晒干。你会在杯子下面看到一层白白的盐。

盐有什么用处呢？我们的生活离不开盐。盐可以让饭菜变得更美味、可口，我们的身体也需要盐才能变得健康。

13

盐可以用来洗东西。盐可以消毒、杀菌。还有人用盐水刷牙、漱口。

冬天下雪的时候，人们会把盐洒在路上，雪落到有盐的地上会融化得更快。

你知道吗?盐还可以用来灭火呢!

你还知道盐有哪些用处呢?

Glossary

	Pinyin	English Definition
海水	hǎi shuǐ	seawater
咸	xián	salty
岩石	yán shí	rock
土壤	tǔ rǎng	soil
盐	yán	salt
溶解	róng jiě	to dissolve
河流	hé liú	river
海洋	hǎi yáng	ocean
蒸发	zhēng fā	to evaporate
留	liú	to leave
盐度	yán dù	salinity
浮力	fú lì	bouyancy
神奇	shén qí	amazing
死海	sǐ hǎi	the Dead Sea
躺	tǎng	to lie down

	Pinyin	English Definition
沉	chén	to sink
实验	shí yàn	experiment
晒	shài	to bask in / to shine on sunshine
干	gān	dry
一层	yì céng	one layer
用处	yòng chu	usefulness
消毒	xiāo dú	to sanitize
杀菌	shā jūn	to sterilize
刷牙	shuā yá	to brush teeth
漱口	shù kǒu	to rinse mouth
洒	sǎ	to sprinkle
融化	róng huà	melt
灭火	miè huǒ	extinguish a fire

www.ingramcontent.com/pod-product-compliance
Lightning Source LLC
Chambersburg PA
CBHW041223070526
44584CB00001B/67